In This Light

Ashley Celeste

BookLeaf
Publishing

India | USA | UK

Made with ❤ on the BookLeaf Publishing Platform
www.bookleafpub.in
www.bookleafpub.com

Dedication

To the poets who are out with lanterns, looking for themselves. You are worth the search.

Preface

These poems were written over the course of several
years,
in my loopy hybrid cursive-print,
oftentimes slanted or scratched on scraps of paper,
tucked into my journals to be lost forever.
Forgotten.

In putting this book together, I was challenged
to rediscover myself through my past writing,
deciphering my emotions
to find my way back to myself.

These poems were written on trains,
in the mountains and along rivers,
on traveling adventures with my daughters,
at home during the pandemic.

But mostly,
they were written by a girl who lost herself
somewhere between marriage and motherhood,
now a woman trying to regain her
sense of self.

Acknowledgements

To my daughters, who inspire me daily and are my continual muses.
To my mom, the original woman of strength in my life.
To every woman writer and poet to have come before me.

The Open Gate

She thinks with her body.
She has to move, to run.
She cannot sit still.

When she reads aloud, she sways
to the rhythm of the words.

She has beautiful skin
and clear, cool eyes.
She is alive and out for the hunt.

Before you can find her, she is gone.
She will take off her shoes
and run barefoot in the grass.

She leaves the gate open,
and the pot of sweet mint near her
tips over, crushing the leaves.

She cannot understand
for the life of her
why others are disrupted by her presence.

She is only seeking happiness

after all. Who could blame her
for that? Who keeps track of her wreckage?

The air smells of mint in her wake,
and only the gate predicts her
coming or going.

Spring Fox
after Mary Oliver

Out there, a fox has risen
from sleep and is staring
at the horizon. She exists
in the field behind my house,
past the lilacs.

Her tail slides between branches-
an orange ghost listening.
There is only one question I have:
how to be free in this world
and still be loved.

I think of her running
swift as the wind,
shedding burdens as she goes.

Whatever else
my life is
with its work,
and its weight and its worry,

it is also this swift shadow
fleeting across fields and brooks;

fiercely free.

All day I think of her -
her orange fur
that doesn't quite blend in,
her roaming, her refusal to be

caught. Somehow,
somehow. This is
my way out,
if only I had her perfect
elusiveness.

Old Town, Albuquerque
March 2019

The man on his woven blanket tells me about praying
for the buffalo to arrive and the snow to pass
or was it the other way around?
His words hold mystery and I cling to them.

Around us, trees blossom in white whispering puffs,
tulips sprout in yellow screaming petals
pressed up against the adobe walls.
Shhhh, I tell the flowers. *Keep yourself a secret.*

He shakes his head in a quiet dissent.
All things we think we understand, we do not.
We are unable to comprehend, he says,
so we misinterpret the message.

Be careful to speak on behalf of someone else,
especially if you assume their silence is a choice.
It often isn't.

Everything we want, he reminds me,
will come in its own time. The snow, the buffalo.
All the moments I wish to trap
will eventually break free and leave.

Just watch the flowers as they bloom
with riotous color, despite the lingering winter cold.

Just watch as my daughters
lose their babyness one day at a time.

Just watch as the spring clouds release
the snow that was previously meant for winter.

The man laughs at me, I think.
Nature is never a secret.
Nothing in this life was meant to be kept.

To the Woman on the Train

A man whispers *stay with me*
which also means
I know you'll never leave.

What angered me is this:
either way
he is right.

We pass a horse tied to an old bridge,
the brackish river underneath it
is moving nowhere.

How long did I think of this leather between us
as reins
when actually
it was no more than a leash.

To the woman on the train:
the most important place in the world
isn't where somebody else forces you to be.

To the woman on the train:
find somewhere you can move
and live without restraint.

To the woman on the train, who is also me:
choose a person who makes the rope of intimacy
feel like a tool for rescue,
not a tool for restraint.

New Year's Day

I press my hand against your chest,
a key into its lock.

We can't undo this.
We have opened Pandora's box.

Mother called me home, and the door
led to darkness.

So I went back to her, eyes down,
avoiding the spun gold of the stars just out of reach:
the stars of what I could've - maybe possibly-
become.

When did I say I wanted a wild life?
When did I long to run free?

The idea strikes as lightning
and is gone just as fast. Stars fall
like moths against the glass pane-

fly up, only to fall again.

Every day I've ever known has been closed to me.

There was never a safe path out of here,
never a compass pointed to a brighter day.

The beautiful daylight hours have lapsed,
a constant reminder that I am but an animal:

a hopeless moth without flight,
wild, without majesty,
all the world's my cage.

Falling From the Apple Tree

At some point
every road becomes two, naturally,
as if the apple could drop from its tree without rotting,
as if the wishbone was never meant to stay whole.

This is the denial that splits us:
one of us believes leaving is necessary.
One believes it is not.

We become invisible to the other, squinting as we search
the horizon, squinting to find what's been lost
as the distance between us widens and
widens again.

You are out there, surely as I am.
Would we recognize the other?
Who plucked us by the scruff of our necks
only to drop us on such opposite paths?

We cannot know. The bone split itself
and crumbled in our hands.
Whose wishes were granted if not our own?

Who in this life receives everything they hope for:

the one who dreams the loudest
or the one who is heard first?

A single foot forward, then the other,
we walk through orchards
on roads of our own making.

We walk to the sounds that suit us now:
your song is light as air, the trees about you growing
easily.
My song tastes of rotted fruit, brambles twisting toward
forever.

Under the Junipers of Taos

When you talk to me about the mountains,
I know if you move any closer to them
I'll never see you again.

The longer you speak about rivers,
the greener your eyes become
and I know that I've lost you.

Then I wonder what, if anything,
you'll be leaving behind.
I see the cracked dirt outside every window,
the dust that covers our reflection in every mirror.

You were never meant for this desert landscape.
Like geese, you will go to find water and fresh air;
those great heights, those distant clouds.

I will stay back and remember that one night in January,
singing together under blankets, near the fire.
We were close once. *Weren't we?*
You knew me too. *Didn't you?*

That winter night, shadows danced across your face
and the stars, oh the stars, how they fell into the

junipers.

Your voice sounded so far away already,
but mine echoed off the adobe,
the saddest thing I've ever heard.

The Smoke Follows

I don't want to leave this place, she said.
Neither do I, sweet daughter.

But long after we're home and the bedding
has been washed and the sleeping bags
have been shelved for the year, I lean in to kiss her
goodnight and inhale deeply, the campfire smell
still clings to the roots of her hair,
to the roots of us.

I am reminded that no matter where we sleep,
the same constellations revolve above us, even if
we can't always see them, even if
the clouds or city lights block our view.

I'm reminded that the memories of a place
are just as important as the place itself.

Those mountains live inside us, sweet girl.
Those rivers and trees have taken root.
They are the root of you.

Sunflowers, 2017

That August, we camped
by the river in Cotopaxi
and slept with our children
between us. The stars fell
into the trees above. The wind
came up the mountain, into the fields
around us, telling me something
urgent. I was radiantly happy.
The sunflowers in the grass turned toward us.
The whole world nudged me, it seemed,
in a wordless fashion, shouting
this is love, shouting
this is your moment, love.
Here, now.

To Grace in Late Summer

Let me imagine a time again-
a time you were just born and it was late
summer.

Let me imagine us no older, when
grief was an empty jar on the windowsill;
joy a white candle, just lit.

Life swelled around us like the summer
monsoon clouds. Gauzy. Tangible.
Our ancient role of *Mother* and *Daughter*,
the sacred circle we held ourselves within.

We lived in the dark then, storms around us,
the smell of rain refreshing the earth.

In the afternoon, you slept
and I had never been more raptured.
We left the windows open back then,
the light from the garden filtering through
the curtains.

Our time was both
ever-long and ever-quick.

Precious hours of astonishment.
Your blinking eyes absorbing the world,
my arms so heavy, so full of you.

Our room that summer was
always scented like an approaching storm.
Your hair always smelled of rain.

To Harper in Early Autumn

Little poet, speak to me.
Your shadows, your storms, your dark
rivers, your up-all-nights,
your windowless dreams.
I long for all your stories.

Little poet, tell me
of the green hills you walk
with your little white dog
trailing behind,
the marigolds bouncing,
the circling light of the sun,
the small truths of you.

Little poet, I cannot find you
without your breadcrumbs.
Leave me a path
so I can see this world
through your eyes.

Little poet, rise like the moon
or set like the sun,
your choice.
Be the night

or be the day,
it matters not.
We exist in a world
lit by you.

Use your words and tell me.
Use your words and speak.
I await.

The Ides of March

Every time I feel close
to understanding the world,
the dryer sounds
and I rise, attending to it with annoyance
and with the pleasure
of a freshly laundered bed.
This is what it's like to live in March,
or perhaps always (*an unconvincing word-*
always) in any context.

Every time I leave my house,
it's with a mix of dread and anticipation.
Is it possible to be the outcast
in your own marriage
and yet be truly (*another untrusting word-*
truly) content alone?

Unable to answer
the questions of my life,
I get up and out, to feel the wind,
my life backed against it,
and know it's time for the trees to bloom
and the grass to sprout.
Never (*one final uncompromising word-*

never) is love as predictable
as this wild earth.

The wind may be anticipated this time of year.
Spring may arrive on schedule.
The laundry will get done.

Can I prepare myself to leave?
But how can I force myself to stay?
Does he care either way?

These, the unknowns of March.

New Moon in Gemini

Language is a spell
and I've trained my words
like little dogs.

See how they run from me
when I've commanded them to stay?

Perhaps I am magic
but have rejected the spells.
Maybe I've forgotten
that magic requires a decisive action.

Should I wander
out into the night
holding a lantern
lit from my altar's flame
and search for myself
between the pines and
among the violets?

These stars are signals
that magic is mine
or at least will be once more.

If I can remember
myself.
If I can stay true
to words within,
and let me take me
to where the magic is.

If I am honest enough
to admit
my home is no longer
inside these walls.

The Green Hills Beyond

She spent the day cleaning and discarding the clutter
from her shelves, from her life.

She put out her Peruvian rug
and planted succulents in the Persian pots.
She hung eucalyptus in every room
and washed her bedroom linen.
She opened every window
to let in the light.

When she is sad like this, she makes herself
a salt bath and soaks at night under the moon,
or she walks the green hills beyond
her home, her refuge. No one can find her out there.
The air is clear, and she can breathe again.

When at last her world was in order,
she decided it was time to leave it.
She stacked on her golden bracelets
and as she escaped to the green hills
behind her home, their chime
was the last that was ever heard of her.

Salida, Colorado

There's a poem hidden somewhere
in this evening and I am determined to find it.

Perhaps it's buried deep in our bones
as we step forward,
in the brittle strength of movement, and
in the courage it takes to keep going,
how doing so can break us.
Sometimes.

Perhaps the poem is lurking in the cottonwoods,
the ones we walk beneath,
our hands almost touching.
From our perspective, the branches
nearly reach the stars.
Nearly.

Perhaps it's hidden in the eyes of the black dog,
the one who knows too much, who watches
too closely. Who feels too familiar
already. Did his yellow eyes see us kiss?
Almost.

Perhaps it's how the temperature drops so suddenly

these nights, that our words form crystals in the air
and I can barely see your eyes.
Before I can stop myself, before we follow
our breath-clouds home. Yours or mine?
Before.

There's a poem hidden out here, my dearest.
Is it in the way we love each other so privately?
Is it in the way our love is screaming out loud?

Manitou

Here, the streets are twisted and the houses
balance atop hills like tightrope walkers. Precarious.

Somewhere, *Rhiannon* comes to us
from an open window, the record repeating:
Would you stay if she promised you heaven?
Stevie knows our dilemma.

We find ourselves on a dark porch,
a string of bulb lights overhead. Stark
and exposed, we exist above the clouds.
Our light matters in the dark world.

We are match flames
striking one against the other,
the friction will make heat,
the heat will burn us up,
until we exist as ash.

Will we survive each other,
or will I be lost to you forever,
incinerated, evaporated, gone?

It's cold here in these mountains, even

in midsummer. Tonight, I fall
asleep outside. Will the quilt be enough
to warm me, or can I count on your anger to do so?

Would you stay...

The song replays and hangs
heavily in the air.
Will you stay if I promise you heaven?
Why do I keep hoping you will?

Elementally

Rusted nails hold the wood of this house
together. Safety with him is an illusion.
Ignore him as I do. He matters not.
Meet me deep in the woods
to find who we once were.
I, moth-footed, and you, owl-eyed.
Tell me who I was as a girl,
I'll do the same for you.
We grew up together, after all.
My want for you then is my offering now.
Longing empties me of all else.
I am but a cicada's husk
clinging to the tree of you.
I await your words like they are little treasures:
shells, chunks of quartz, old keys.
The souvenirs of a past life have become
hushed voices over the phone deep into the night.
Will you take me as I am now?
A candle of desire burns in me,
even as my cobwebbed body has all but given up.
In the next room, my husband sleeps.
I've never been more awake, nakedly hoping
that you and I can meet again
in the green hills out back. He won't find us.

I haven't forgotten anything about you. I remember it all.
In this light, you look silver.
Elementally, you are moonlight and memory,
and yet, you are more substantial, my sweet ghost,
than the wooden door I closed softly
to get to you. How, after all these years,
are you able to haunt me so?

Into the Trees

Mom, do I seem bigger to you?
She is so full of questions
once the sun drops and the stars rise,
when sparks from the campfire appear,
slow at first, then all at once.

When we started camping, she was so little that
she held my finger tightly as we walked to the river,
the mud squishing between her chubby toes
still painted glittery pink from her third birthday.
Her baby teeth so white, the green of her eyes
doll-like, absorbing the wilderness. I was always near,
her shadow to chase. Her shadow that tagged along.

So many years later, a decade now past,
I'm haunted by that memory and how
she is still right here, emerging from the juniper woods
to show me pictures of the creek she found nearby.

She doesn't need me now - or at least-
she doesn't need me in the same way.
She is free to explore on nights like this,
taking a lantern, a camera, her sense of adventure.

I move about, unsure of how to be useful.
I am a shadow without a person to cling to,
a little lost, looking to the stars for answers.

Yes, I tell her. *You are getting bigger,*
and to myself I whisper, *You're already gone.*
Having borrowed my shoes to go down to the water,
her footprints and any little pieces of me left
are already disappearing into the trees.

In This Light

I've lived out here too long,
out in the woods and in the rain.
I'm made of fallen leaves and hollow trees;
the moonlight my lacy dress,
the roses my blush.
In every season, an everlasting wonder.

In this light, I know what it is to be me.

Then one night, you lit a fire inside the cabin
and beckoned me,
negotiated a trade, one life for the other.
Was the dowry worth the price?

The woman before you was once a girl
with fingers free to plunge about in the mud
weighed down with neither a diamond nor ring.

That girl vanished as she grew,
her wild abandon locked in a box
and you held the only key.

She became the perfect feast for a wolf.
I traded the wilderness of me for a home with you.

In the middle of the night, you vanished and left me here
alone.

My life has become an origami figure, bending into itself
again and again
until I am unrecognizable to myself
in this light.

I tried to follow you, track you down,
but got lost in the woods of myself.
I scream my name into the wild,
wildly hoping she will answer back.

I long to be the girl you once knew,
the girl you stole in the middle of the night,
the girl who traded her dandelion crown for a veil,
the girl who thought the only danger in these woods
was a wolf, never knowing that in this light
the wolf was you.

Scorpio Season

The prodigal daughter returns
home, if it was ever hers at all,
and the stars arrange themselves
just as her ancestors demanded,
ever-present reminders that
someone at some moment in time
is prompting her
to find a path back
home to herself.

Why are daughters asked
to sacrifice their lives,
to hover near their needy families
who only seek to drown them,
asked to forgive everyone
who have violated their boundaries
egregiously, and then asked
to do so graciously?

Why can daughters look everyone
in the eye except for themselves?

The mirrors stand covered
in her room;

there will be no scrutinizing.
She knows what she's become.

One morning, perhaps not
too distant in the future, she'll awaken
and understand the power
she holds within herself.

She will let her fire leak out of her heart
to give the day its light.

She will immediately stop
trying to keep people
together
who have fallen so tragically
apart.

In this way, she'll come to imagine
a new life for herself, one free of the weight
of others, one free of guilt.

When the abandonment of herself
is over, she will celebrate
her homecoming with wine and feast
and poetry and bonfires.

She will make friends with herself

and find peace to love whom she chooses.
Her time will be hers. Her dreams, too.

Watch how the stars react,
wild and bright across the sky,
once a daughter breaks free.